Original title:
The Orchard's Embrace

Copyright © 2025 Creative Arts Management OÜ
All rights reserved.

Author: Alec Davenport
ISBN HARDBACK: 978-1-80586-311-3
ISBN PAPERBACK: 978-1-80586-783-8

Serenity Among the Fruits

In a grove where apples tease,
Pears are prancing as they please.
Cherries giggle on the vine,
While plums complain, "This sun is mine!"

A grapefruit sings in silly tones,
Trying to charm those orange cones.
Bananas slip and slide with glee,
"Hey, look at me! I'm fruit royalty!"

Berries cozy up, they do,
Whispering secrets like a crew.
Kiwi jokes about his fuzz,
Says, "I'm handsome, just because!"

In this patch, the laughter grows,
When lemons giggle, everyone knows.
Together they dance, a fruity parade,
In their world, all sorrows fade.

The Spirit of Fruition

In a land where apples hide,
Lemons laugh and prunes abide.
Bouncing fruits in silly games,
Whispering each other's names.

Bananas slide on playful peels,
While zesty oranges spin their wheels.
Cherries giggle in the breeze,
Winking at the fluffy bees.

Sunkissed Memories

Underneath the golden sun,
Tomatoes dance, they're having fun.
Peppers prance with silly flair,
Juggling seeds up in the air.

Cucumbers tell a corny tale,
Of veggie races on the trail.
Carrots wear their finest hats,
While radishes throw little chats.

Layers of Life

Onion layers peel with speed,
Each round reveals a different deed.
Garlic shuffles, bold and bright,
Whispering secrets through the night.

Zucchini shows off fancy moves,
Making sure to catch the grooves.
Spinach struts its leafy spin,
While kale giggles, "Let's begin!"

A Palette of Seasons

In spring, the berries burst with cheer,
Dancing petals far and near.
Watermelons wear a smile,
Growing rounder by the mile.

Autumn brings a cornfield rave,
Pumpkins roll, oh how they wave!
Winter settles, crisp and white,
Fruits snuggle in their cozy night.

Roots of Connection

In a garden where laughter grows,
Sunflowers dance, and the wind blows.
A gnome fell off his tiny chair,
Sipping dew, he couldn't help but stare.

Potatoes gossip beneath the ground,
Carrots whisper jokes all around.
The radishes roll, trying to flee,
Oh, what fun - just look and see!

Shadows in the Sunlight

In shadows long, the pears do sneak,
Hiding from sunlight, so bold and sleek.
An apple laughed at a shy green grape,
Together, they planned a cheeky escape.

The bees are buzzing quite a tune,
Stinging humor, beneath the moon.
They danced in circles, quite absurd,
Making friends with a chatty bird!

Heartbeats Under the Leaves

Under the leaves, where secrets hide,
A squirrel cracked jokes with utmost pride.
The acorns chuckled, feeling quite clever,
"Guess who's nuts? We are forever!"

The breeze comes in with silly sighs,
Yes, it tickles all, oh what a surprise!
A symphony of laughter does play,
As critters frolic throughout the day.

Honeyed Mornings

Mornings drip with sweetness, oh what a sight,
Bees take sips of golden light.
The toast pops up with a zany cheer,
While the buttered bread whispers "How's it, dear?"

Jam joins in with a fruity grin,
Tickling the sleepy, where to begin?
The pancakes flip, in a dance so bold,
Serving laughter with syrupy gold!

Bountiful Solitude

In an orchard so bright, I found a pear,
It winked at me; was it trying to share?
I asked it a joke, it rolled off the tree,
Said, "Stop with the puns, just let me be free!"

A cherry chimed in with a giggle so sweet,
"Your jokes are as ripe as my juicy red seat!"
Cider spilled laughter, fresh fruit in a bowl,
Life's fruitiest moments, they make my heart roll.

Intertwined Paths

Beneath the boughs, I danced with a vine,
It teased and it twisted; we both thought we'd shine!
But tripping on roots, I fell in a heap,
A squirrel roared laughing, might wake up the sheep.

With apples all chuckling, they whispered of fate,
"You should try jogging... don't leave us to wait!"
So here in the grove, we tumble and spin,
Even the nuts join in, grinning with sin.

The Veil of Verdance

Among the green leaves, a prankster did lurk,
It tossed down a lemon with a sly kind of smirk.
"Catch me if you can!" it giggled with glee,
I slipped on the juice—oh, what a sight to see!

Peaches rolled past, all in stripes like a thief,
They laughed at my plight, shedding tears of relief.
"Life's too short to fret! Join our fruit party!"
As I joined the fun, I felt quite hearty.

Whispering Fragrance

In the garden of smells, all the fruits had a chat,
Bananas told secrets with a festive old hat.
"Why did the apple lay low on the ground?"
It answered with giggles, "I lost my way 'round!"

Plum glanced at Orange, who rolled his bright eyes,
"You should try my joke, it's a real surprise!"
"Why do grapes never play hide and seek?"
They burst into laughter, their voices unique.

Greener Pastures

In fields where grass is oh so high,
Cows play hopscotch, pigs just fly.
A rogue snail races, oh what a scene,
Who knew grass could be so green?

Chickens gossip about their fate,
While goats debate who's got the weight.
Under the sun, they twirl and prance,
In their world of hay, they all do dance.

The Glow of Abundance

Fruits are hanging, ripe and bright,
Squirrels plot a fruit parade tonight.
An apple sings, a banana jokes,
These fruits have more fun than all the folks.

Berries chatter, making a fuss,
Peaches blush when on a bus.
Watermelons rolling, what a mess,
Each one's a character, nothing less.

Hushed Conversations

Under the trees, whispers collide,
A rabbit with secrets, tries to hide.
A raccoon nods with a cookie in hand,
As if discussing a master plan.

Starlings gossip, swooping so low,
While crickets strike up an evening show.
In the hush, the laughter blooms,
Nature's comedy in vibrant rooms.

Enchanted Heartwood

A tree stump claims its royal seat,
Hosts a gathering, a dance so sweet.
With ants on stilts and bees in hats,
The party's wild, oh how it chats!

Woodpeckers laugh at a clumsy fly,
While tree frogs leap to aim for the sky.
Every branch joins in on the fun,
When wood meets whimsy, all must run!

Embracing the Harvest

When apples fall with a thud,
I dodge to avoid that fruity flood.
The pears are plotting, I swear they're sly,
With every bite, they land a pie.

The pumpkins giggle, they roll with glee,
While I trip over a root, oh, woe is me!
But laughter blooms in the golden light,
As I dance with veggies, what a sight!

Roots and Dreams

The carrots tell tales from deep in the ground,
While lettuce laughs, all crisp and sound.
I dream of pies, oh, what a feat,
But end up munching on tomato's sweet treat.

Potatoes nod, with eyes all around,
As dreams sprout legs and dance on the ground.
The radishes snicker, their tops waving high,
And I join the party, oh me, oh my!

Treading Through the Lush

Butterflies flirt, they tease and they sway,
While I step on daisies, who bark and say,
'Watch where you're treading, you clumsy friend!'
But the flowers just giggle, they never pretend.

Among the green, I weave with delight,
Tripping on grass, oh, what a sight!
The herbs are a laugh, they smell a bouquet,
Chasing my thoughts far, far away!

A Garden's Warmth

Sunflowers wave as they share their cheer,
While the basil rolls jokes that are quite queer.
The tomatoes blush, they're ripe and round,
And the zucchini's dance makes silly sounds.

A garden's warmth, a whimsical dance,
With bugs that waltz, take every chance.
So join in my folly, let spirits soar,
In this veggie kingdom, life's never a bore!

Under the Boughs of Friendship

Beneath the trees where laughter grows,
We share our snacks and funny woes.
A bee just buzzed, it stole my fries,
We laugh as it buzzes and quickly flies.

The branches sway with our silly grins,
Count the apples—whoever wins!
With every bite, we're filled with cheer,
Tell that squirrel to disappear!

Reaping Joys of the Heart

We gather fruit, it's quite the sight,
An apple fell—no need for fright!
We dance around with fruit on heads,
And laugh so hard, fall in the spreads.

The harvest time brings us great delight,
Wobbling thoughts take sudden flight.
Giggles echo through the shade,
Where sticky hands leave fun displayed.

Symphony of the Orchard

Can you hear the sound of the crunch?
A symphony while we munch and munch!
The birds join in with their wild songs,
  While we invent the silliest wrongs.

Fruits jive and tumble, hitting the ground,
With squeals and laughs, joy's supreme sound.
  Oh what a ruckus, what a show,
    Against the trees, antics flow!

Ripened Moments

As the sun dips low, we plot and scheme,
Making sweet moments, living the dream.
A frisbee flies, a fruit flies too,
Loaded with laughter, our friendship grew.

The shadows stretch like a silly dance,
We take a tumble, then hop at chance.
With every bruise, joy's fruit we bear,
Ripened connection, beyond compare.

Sunkissed Silhouettes

In the sun we strive to tan,
But end up sporting farmer's plans.
With fruit hats perched in comical style,
We giggle and hug, stay a while.

Bees buzz around in awkward flight,
Chasing us from morning till night.
We shimmy in shadows, all in good cheer,
While squawking birds bring our laughter near.

Ripe with Memory

Each fruit we pluck tells a tale,
Of silly pranks and minor fails.
The apples roll, the pears collide,
As laughter bursts, we take it in stride.

Funny faces, juice-stained lips,
We try to juggle with wild flips.
Fruits like clowns, they slip and slide,
Creating chaos we can't abide.

Dance of the Petals

Petals swirl like confetti in flight,
We twirl and spin, what a sight!
With each misstep, we burst into glee,
Flapping like ducks, wild and free.

In the breeze, our hair's a mess,
Branches tease with playful finesse.
We dance like stars on clumsy legs,
Tripping over roots, like playful pegs.

Echoes in the Grove

Laughter echoes through leafy lanes,
Chasing giggles like runaway trains.
With each echo, a smile blooms wide,
As goofy antics we can't hide.

Squirrels stare with raised eyebrows,
As we strike poses, all the hows!
In this grove, every moment's fun,
Dancing shadows in the setting sun.

The Lure of Sweetness

In the trees, the fruits all laugh,
A pear stole a joke from the grape,
The apples rolled their eyes in glee,
While cherries danced in fruity shape.

A banana slipped on his peel,
Said, 'I swear I'm on solid ground!'
The oranges shook in citrus joy,
As laughter spread all around.

With every bite, they crack a pun,
Each berry winks, so round and bright,
They know their sweetness is a hit,
And play all day, from morn till night.

So gather 'round, let's share a bite,
The fruits will tell you tales so bold,
In this garden of snickers sweet,
Where secrets of laughter unfold.

Abiding Shadows

Underneath the leafy greens,
A butternut squash finds a bed,
He hums a tune to his friends near,
While zucchini keeps tapping its head.

A tomato blushed, oh what a sight,
'Tis just the sun,' said a sly sprout,
But veggies all know the truth it hides,
That laughter's what it's really about!

The shadows sway with funny quirks,
As carrots chat with beats so tight,
In the coolness, they joke and play,
Until the day turns into night.

So if you wander through this patch,
Listen closely, hear them cheer,
For beneath the very greenest leaves,
Are shadows that tickle and endear.

Heartfelt Offerings

With baskets full of silly dreams,
The fruits parade with colors bright,
A fruity fair of joy and charm,
As smiles take flight in the daylight.

A raspberry winked at a peach,
While a fig tried to tell a tale,
They shared their hopes upon a vine,
That humor would always prevail.

A breeze blew soft with playful whispers,
Caressing each branch and leaf,
While laughter rolled like ripened grapes,
Bringing joy and sweet relief.

So join this feast of silly love,
Where each fruit makes its claim,
In the gathering of the heart,
Laughter's the sweetest game.

Nectar of Togetherness

In the sunlight, each fruit shines bright,
Bananas in a friendly line,
They plot a prank on a shy plum,
Who's too sweet to decline.

An apple named Fred wore a hat,
While pears giggled at his style,
'They say that I'm just peel and core,'
He chuckled, with a funny smile.

From blossoms came the nectar's laugh,
As bees buzzed in a merry trance,
Pollinating all the fun here,
Encouraging a silly dance.

So grab a fruit, let's toast our joy,
United in this summer's zest,
In the garden of goofy sweetness,
Where togetherness is the best!

A Refuge of Growth

Under the trees, a squirrel dances,
Chasing its tail in funny prances.
A bird snickers from a nearby bough,
"You'll never catch it!" it sings with a vow.

Sunlight spills like honey on leaves,
While worms conspire, wearing their sleeves.
Beehives buzz with gossip galore,
"Who knew the daisies would ask for more?"

Rabbits gossip in whispering throngs,
"Have you tasted the apples? They're mostly wrong!"
But beneath the laughter, roots explore,
Growing friendships, forevermore.

Each fruit a joke, ripe with delight,
Pick one! It's bound to give you a fright.
Nature's chuckle in every bite,
Makes the day funny, oh so bright!

The Beauty of Borrowed Time

Time ticks slow under leafy shrouds,
Where moments giggle, drawing crowds.
An acorn drops, a chipmunk swears,
"I borrowed this!" it silently declares.

The clock's hands spin in a wild jig,
While bumblebees buzz like a jolly gig.
"Time's a thief," says a prancing hare,
"But we're all late, who really cares?"

Cherry blossoms bloom with a cheer,
"Remember the time we forgot last year?"
They toss petals like confetti in spring,
Laughing at the trouble time can bring.

With each pink swirl, a tale unfolds,
Rich with the laughter that nature holds.
Borrowed moments, so quick to rhyme,
What's sweeter than life in borrowed time?

Nectar of Tranquility

In a patch of clover, a caterpillar smiles,
Sipping nectar for miles and miles.
A snail on a leaf cracks a joke,
"I'm just here for the nectar, no need to poke!"

Butterflies burst into giggling flight,
Fluttering wings in the warm sunlight.
"Who knew flowers had such wild dreams?"
They sip the nectar, or so it seems.

A ladybug rolls, laughing out loud,
"Nature's a party, come join the crowd!"
Bees buzz with laughter, weaving their song,
"Who needs the gym when you dance along?"

In each drop lies a whimsical thrill,
Nature's nectar, a taste to fulfill.
With every sip, tranquility found,
A funny dance where all are unbound!

Gardens of Connection

In the garden, friends plant their dreams,
Tending to laughter, or so it seems.
A root peers out, gives a cheeky grin,
"You can't plant hope with a frown for a chin!"

A wheelbarrow giggles rolling away,
Spilling soil in a happy display.
"Oh my!" says a flower, bright and spry,
"What a mess, but we'll let it fly!"

Garden gnomes trade tales at night,
About the antics of worms in flight.
"Did you hear they're all in a race?"
"No way! They're just keeping up with pace!"

Flowers share secrets under the moon,
Buzzing with joy, they hum a tune.
In dirt and laughter, a bond we find,
In gardens of connection, laughter entwined!

A Sanctuary of Color and Light

In the garden, colors blend,
Silly bees dance without end.
A squirrel steals a shiny treat,
As flowers giggle under feet.

Sunlight splashes, shadows play,
A worm winks in a cheeky way.
The trees wear hats of blooming cheer,
And daisies whisper, 'Spring is here!'

A butterfly trips on a vine,
While rabbits sip on grape divine.
Laughter blooms in every breeze,
As nature sings with perfect ease.

With every fruit, a joke is told,
And stories of the brave and bold.
In this place of whimsy bright,
Where joy and color bring delight.

Harmony in Nature's Garden

In the garden, tunes abound,
Singing chickens, such a sound!
A cat decides to join the throng,
And meows along with nature's song.

The flowers sway, they start to groove,
While butterflies break into a move.
A frog croaks out a silly beat,
As worms tap dance beneath the heat.

Birds wear hats, all decked in flair,
While grasshoppers jump without a care.
Laughter echoing, pure delight,
Nature's party, a true highlight!

A chilly breeze, the music swells,
Each petal's laugh, a story tells.
In this garden, harmony reigns,
Where whimsy spills like summer rains.

Scent of Promise in the Air

The aroma wafts, oh what a tease,
As cupcakes bloom among the trees!
A skunk strolls by, all dressed in style,
With a fragrance that's worth a while.

Roses chuckle, scenting the sky,
While daisies wink as bees fly by.
A perfume mix that's quite bizarre,
With minty hopes and chocolate bars.

Lemon whiffs with laughter play,
While pears giggle in their own way.
The breeze brings whispers of sweet treats,
As nature serves up fun delights, not feats.

Under the sun, smells twist and twirl,
A feast of scents in a whimsical whirl.
In this air of slight dismay,
Even the doughnuts seem to sway!

Reflections Among the Blossoms

In the pond, the flowers preen,
While frogs pretend to be the queen.
A duck quacks out a silly tune,
And twirls beneath the smiling moon.

Blossoms mirror every grin,
With petals dancing, let's begin!
The fish poke fun at their own fins,
As laughter bubbles, joy begins.

A turtle struts, just like a star,
While dragonflies zoom near and far.
In this water, fun takes a dive,
And silly antics come alive!

Beneath the blooms, reflections play,
As nature pulls odd tricks all day.
With giggles echoing through the glass,
Life's a party, let moments pass!

The Secret Life of Trees

In the garden, whispers grow,
Trees in coats of green now show.
With roots that dance beneath the ground,
They giggle softly, making sound.

Squirrels plot and pinecones scheme,
Trees hold secrets, it would seem.
Branches wave like hands in glee,
"Look at me, could I be a bee?"

Under moonlight, they take flight,
Falling leaves, a comic sight.
A rough bark with stories grand,
Leaves act in a leafy band.

So next time you stroll right past,
Remember trees have fun amassed.
In the silence of foliage so keen,
Lies laughter waiting to be seen.

Gift of the Fruiting Tree

A tree once wore a fruiting cap,
With apples round and juicy, in a nap.
"Bite me now!" said one in red,
The pear chimed in, "I'll taste better instead!"

Cherries giggled from their stems,
While plums were plotting fruity ems.
Bananas slipped, oh what a game,
They laughed about their silly name.

One windy day, the fruits took flight,
Riding breezes, oh what a sight!
With laughter trailing in the breeze,
"Catch us if you can, if you please!"

In the basket, they all collide,
A fruity party, none can hide.
So when you munch on what's so sweet,
Remember fruits know how to greet!

Whispering Leaves and Hidden Paths

The leaves are chattering in their place,
Exchanging gossip at a fast pace.
"Did you hear 'bout that branch's bend?"
"Oh, he's been swaying since last weekend!"

A squirrel skips down hidden trails,
With acorns tucked in funny pails.
He pauses for a chat, quite spry,
"The grasshopper thought he could fly!"

Through rustling shades, the laughter flows,
Wind tickles cheeks, as friendship grows.
The roots below keep secrets tight,
Among the trees, it's pure delight.

So follow paths where whispers lead,
In green embrace, hearts truly feed.
Just don't forget to laugh a tad,
For nature's humor's always glad!

The Lullaby of Ripening

As moons glow bright, the fruits do sigh,
In a cradle of leaves, they lie.
A peach hums low, a gentle tune,
While cherries dance beneath the moon.

Ripening dreams on summer's breath,
Each fruit claims joy like a play of chess.
Grapes giggle as they roll around,
Making merry with the sounds they found.

With morning dew, they stretch and yawn,
Sweet nectar forming, energy drawn.
They play peek-a-boo with the sun,
In this fruity world, everyone has fun!

So raise a glass to all that grows,
With playful spirits, this life bestows.
In the orchard, there's no lack,
Of laughter sweet, it calls you back!

Sunlit Reverie

In a garden where giggles bloom,
Fruit trees wear a sunny costume.
The apples are pranksters, oh what a sight,
With glimmers of mischief, they twinkle in light.

A pear tried to dance, slipped on its skin,
While the cherries were laughing, just joining in.
The sun winked down, in laughter we bask,
What kind of fruit would dare to ask?

A melon recited a joke so fine,
But the oranges rolled, they weren't on time.
With juice-filled laughter that tickled the breeze,
In this bright spot, we're all feeling pleased.

So let's pluck this joy as we reach for the sky,
With every fruit's chuckle, oh me, oh my!
In this vivid scene, we laugh and we dream,
In sunshine-soaked moments, we're part of the team.

Cradle of Abundance

Under boughs where the squirrels play,
Fruits giggle softly throughout the day.
Bananas wear bows, the berries wear hats,
And couple of cucumbers chill with the cats.

An avocado told me it's feeling quite grand,
Wiggling its seeds as it started a band.
The melody's ripe with a humorous twist,
Can you hear the laughter? You wouldn't want to miss!

With laughter like nectar, sweet in the air,
The tomatoes are blushing, quite unaware.
They'll roll on their backs, through the fields they'll roam,
In this cradle of fun, we're never alone.

Oh, what a gathering, such frolics abound,
As the fruits leap and giggle, a whimsical sound.
In this odd little corner, we find our delight,
In a cradle of abundance, our hearts feel light.

The Soul of the Harvest

Gather 'round, it's harvest time,
With dancing pumpkins, oh so prime.
The squash is smirking with all its might,
While the corn ears chatter, ready to delight.

The grapes are gossiping, sweet and sly,
As they dangle by, waving hi.
A cabbage rolls in, what a sight to see,
With arms outstretched, it's so much glee.

A carrot shared secrets, buried deep,
While the turnips giggled, they couldn't keep.
In this humorous, hearty harvest spree,
Every veggie joins in for raucous glee.

Let's toast to this feast with a wink and a cheer,
For the soul of the harvest is laughter so clear.
With each playful chuckle, the season ignites,
In this joyful gather, our spirit takes flight.

A Mosaic of Color

In the patchwork field, colors collide,
Pumpkins in orange with smiles so wide.
The turnips wear purple, so grand and chic,
While the peppers throw parties that last for a week.

A salad of laughter, tossed all around,
With the radishes giggling, they dance on the ground.
A rainbow of humor graced by the sun,
In this vivid mosaic, everyone's fun.

Lettuce had layers, with jokes woven tight,
While the beets turned red, out of sheer delight.
It's a vibrant display with the fruits and the greens,
In this patch of laughter, we're living our dreams.

So let's celebrate color, let's sing and let's play,
For the joy of the harvest unfolds every day.
In this mosaic so bright, our spirits will soar,
With nature's own laughter, forever we'll explore.

Fruitful Whispers

In a world of juicy pears,
The secrets float with flair.
A squirrel danced, quite absurd,
Chasing shadows, not a word.

Bananas giggle on the tree,
Tickling lemons, oh what glee!
Grapes hold puns, unjipeared,
While apples roll and seem quite scared.

The breeze tells jokes, a playful tease,
With cherries laughing in the breeze.
Bumblebees buzz, wearing tiny hats,
Like little stand-up, furry spats.

If laughter's fruit hangs on each bough,
Then here's the punchline, take a bow!
In this garden, joy's the key,
Beneath the fruit, let's plant a tree.

Boughs of Serenity

Under branches, laughs collide,
Where watermelons bloom with pride.
Peaches grinning, ripe and sweet,
Making mischief with their seat.

Lemons spin like plates on high,
Frolicking under the vast sky.
A coconut's joke falls flat,
As avocados chat with a splat!

Each leaf rustles, tale of light,
Honeyed laughs brighten the night.
Cider dreams with sparkling flair,
Even the crickets join the air.

So sit and giggle, won't you stay?
Fruitful fun in a fanciful way.
The boughs aren't just for hanging treats,
But for jests and joyful feats.

Beneath the Canopy's Glow

Beneath the leaves, where shadows play,
An orange juggles through the day.
Bananas slip on silken toes,
Finding humor in their woes.

A limping pear makes quite the scene,
Wobbling past a brisk machine.
Raspberries laugh in playful chatter,
While plums debate on what's the matter.

Grapefruit grins, a cheeky chap,
Telling jokes that make hearts clap.
Moments burst with fruity cheer,
Watermelons cracked from laughter here.

Underneath this vibrant dome,
Delightful whispers find a home.
Each fruit's grin, a gift to share,
In this funny world, life lays bare.

Harvesting Dreams

In fields of dreams where fruits unite,
The cherries giggle, oh so bright.
Watermelons prank as they roll,
Tickling toes, that's their goal.

The corn takes bets on the next big splash,
While berries cheer in a vibrant clash.
With every vine, a story's spun,
And autumn's dance has just begun.

Fruits whisper tales of past disgrace,
As pumpkins pose with comic grace.
Peppers pop with stories bold,
Revealing laughter, tales retold.

So come, dear friend, let's toast and cheer,
To nature's wonder, loud and clear.
In this harvest, joy's supreme,
With every bite, we're living dreams.

A Haven of Petals

In fields where daisies plot,
The bees employ a silly dance.
With petals swirling, laughter's caught,
A bug in pants? What a chance!

Sunshine jokes and shadows tease,
Squirrels wear their acorn hats.
A cherry tree sways in the breeze,
Whispering secrets to the bats.

Under branches, we all play,
Chasing shadows, laughing loud.
The sun takes off at end of day,
We wave goodbye, quite over-proud.

Humidity's a funny friend,
With sticky hugs that make us grin.
We'll run and spin 'til daylight's end,
In our petal haven, we win!

The Dance of Blossoms

Giggles float on breezy air,
As blossoms twirl and trip along.
Each petal has a secret flair,
Humor's woven in their song.

A butterfly forgot its route,
And lands upon a lady's hat.
She laughs, purses her lips to pout,
Mystified by nature's spat.

The trees break out in ticklish glee,
A branch supports a squirrel's dive.
In every nook, it's plain to see,
Nature's folly helps us thrive.

So grab a friend, let's take a whirl,
As petals float like giggly pearls.
In every dance of this bright world,
We find the joy that freely unfurls.

Sweet Surrender of Seasons

Fruits giggle as they ripen their ways,
Cherries sneak in candy coats.
Apples whisper, "We'll get your gaze,"
While raspberries dance in silly boats.

Leaves play hide and seek in blushing hues,
Each gust of wind, a playful toss.
They swirl in whirls of colorful shoes,
"Who needs a compass? We're the boss!"

While pumpkins plot their Halloween glee,
The squash is working on its riddle.
"Just wait," it says with mischievous glee,
"I'll show you how to dance on the middle!"

So seasons bounce and skip around,
Life's funny quirks kept all aglow.
In every bite of sweetness found,
Nature's humor steals the show!

Shelter of Fruits and Memories

Beneath the tree's wide, leafy arms,
Lemons giggle, sour and sweet.
They trade sunshine for playful charms,
Creating lemonade with every greet.

A picnic blankets spread with glee,
Sandwiches giggling with pickle power.
Each fruit has tales to share, you see,
As we tease the ants that try to flower.

Quirky laughs from nature's shelf,
As melon bombs burst from sweet bites.
Every laughter echoes like a elf,
In this bounty, joy ignites.

So rally round, let's share a toast,
To fruits that hold our sweetest dreams.
In this wild garden, we'll boast,
Of tasty fun and laughter's beams!

Shelter in Solitude

In the shade of trees so wise,
I told my secrets to the flies.
They buzzed back with thoughts quite grand,
Like a crazy, buzzing band.

A squirrel basked, ate my snack,
He winked at me, then took a crack.
I laughed so hard, I lost my seat,
Rolling down, oh what a feat!

Dancing leaves did a jig of glee,
While I wondered, 'What's wrong with me?'
Nature's odd jesters laugh and play,
In solitude, I found my way.

Here in quiet, with critters around,
Life is silly; joy I've found.
With each giggle that takes its start,
The world seems lighter on my heart.

Whispers Underneath

Roots grumble low, with tales to share,
About a frog with fancy hair.
He croaked a song that made me smile,
I stopped to listen for a while.

The worms debated who's the best,
One's fancy suit put them to jest.
They wriggled, jiggled, made a scene,
A fashion show that was unseen.

Beneath the leaves, the laughter swirled,
Even the crickets joined this world.
They chirped their tunes, quite offbeat,
In this odd dance, no one's discreet.

Who would think, in silence found,
Such wacky whispers all around?
Nature's party, unplanned, it seems,
In the shadows, we live our dreams.

The Lilt of Leaves

Leaves are gossiping something sweet,
About the bird who lost his seat.
He flapped his wings and flew so high,
But landed hard, oh me, oh my!

The breeze joined in with a chuckle,
As nuts and berries formed a huddle.
"I'll tell you tales of silly birds,"
Said the acorn, as he stirred.

A dance began upon the ground,
With twigs and fruits, they spun around.
Laughter echoed through the trees,
In this grove, such joy does tease!

Here we gather, as nature sings,
With every rustle, laughter springs.
The lilt of leaves, a soft delight,
Cracking jokes until the night.

A Gathering of Spirits

In the cool, crisp air at dusk,
The shadows gather, smell of musk.
Ghostly figures play hide and seek,
With the wise old owl, quite unique.

They boogie down, the phantoms sway,
What a party! Come join their fray.
Bumbling and tumbling, they roll about,
Ghostly giggles echo, no doubt!

Mushrooms wink under moonlit glare,
As fog conceals this wild affair.
What a sight, what a sound,
In the night, laughter does abound.

Each spirit's tale is quite a trip,
With antics that make your heart skip.
In this gathering, joy's the bone,
Turn the dark into a happy zone.

Sowing Seeds of Kindness

In the garden of giggles, we plant our cheer,
With each tiny seed, laughter draws near.
We water with joy and sunlight so bright,
Growing smiles by day, tickles by night.

The worms dance in soil, doing cha-cha,
While the bees hum along to their own sweet aria.
A squirrel with a hat takes a cheeky leap,
Spreading goodwill in a way that's quite deep.

The Scent of Ripeness

Fruits hang like lanterns, bright and round,
Mangoes and peaches, in sweetness they're bound.
A banana slips by, with a flick and a slide,
Leaving us chuckling, we can't help but hide.

The berries gossip in their juicy attire,
While apples debate who's the juiciest sire.
The laughter of harvest, a colorful spree,
In this comical patch, we're all family.

Beneath the Sweet Canopy

Here we dance under trees with a playful sway,
Kicking up leaves that twirl and play.
The branches overhead are like jokes unspooled,
Each rustle a punchline, nature's rules!

A parrot pop quizzes with feathers so bright,
As he squawks out jokes, oh what a sight!
We sip on the nectar, a funny elixir,
While snickering squirrels take turns as the fixer.

Cradled by Nature's Hands

In the arms of green, we find quite the charm,
Bouncing on boughs, there's never a harm.
A frog croaks a tune, like a bad karaoke,
While turtles groove slowly, feeling quite smokey.

Each leaf tells a story, with whispers and cheers,
Nature's big laugh echoes through the years.
With sun on our faces and fun all around,
In this buzzing retreat, joy's always found.

Journeys Among the Growing Shadows

Beneath the trees we share our snacks,
Squirrels steal fries, they're little hacks.
We trade our snacks for silly bets,
Dancing with shadows, making debts.

A peach fell down, it hit my head,
I laughed so hard, forgot my bread.
The sunlight tickles through the leaves,
Nature's laughter never grieves.

The shadows grow as we share tales,
Of secret paths and silly fails.
We trip on roots and giggle loud,
Who knew nature could be such a crowd?

With every bite, we make a face,
Fruit juice is such a sticky race.
We cheer for all the silly pranks,
In nature's playground, giving thanks.

Embracing Nature's Cycle

In springtime blooms, we hop and play,
Join bees in dances, bright bouquet.
A flower hat, my head it wears,
Whirling like a bee with pairs.

The trees hold secrets, can you hear?
The rustling leaves, a giggle near.
With funny faces, we chase the breeze,
Nature's laugh whispers through the trees.

We pluck ripe fruits, they land like bombs,
Smushed by feet in nature's qualms.
Every squishy step is a delight,
Who knew apples could make such a fight?

As seasons change, we laugh and dance,
Nature throws a wonky chance.
We twirl in circles, arms held wide,
In the cycle's hug, we take pride.

Fruits of Serenity

A pear for lunch, a peach for fun,
In fruit salad, we see the sun.
With each bright slice, a giggle flies,
Splashing juice like rainbow skies.

Oh, cherries bounce like tiny glee,
Slipping on juice, oh woe is me!
But laughter's sweeter than any pie,
We feast on joy, that's no lie.

We dress the fruits in silly hats,
And let them dance, oh how they chat!
Plum winks at lime, it's quite the sight,
In this funny fruit-filled twilight.

When the feast is done, we must depart,
With sticky hands and grateful heart.
Each bite's a joke that nature made,
In every fruit, our laughter laid.

Whispers Amongst the Boughs

The branches sway, they start to tease,
Rustling whispers ride the breeze.
What secrets hide in leafy folds?
Funny stories yet untold.

We climb to heights of silly dreams,
Making crowns from apples' gleams.
Each branch a stage for monkey plays,
We laugh till dusk, through sunny rays.

The boughs above start to gossip loud,
While we perform before a crowd.
The squirrels cheer, the birds applaud,
For every nutty joke we trod.

As twilight nears, our show concludes,
Leaving laughter in the woods' moods.
We shout goodnight to leafy friends,
In whispers of joy, the fun never ends.

A Tapestry of Green and Gold

In a garden wild and bright,
Where the squirrels dance with delight.
A rabbit hops, oh what a sight,
Wearing carrots, feeling quite right.

The apples giggle on their boughs,
Sharing secrets with the cows.
The bees are buzzing, oh my how,
They're breaking bread, take a bow.

Chasing shadows, what a chase,
A chicken slips, falls from grace.
The pumpkins roll in a jovial race,
While little ones laugh, embrace the space.

With a twist and a turn, they play,
Fruits and veggies join the fray.
In this weird, whimsical way,
Joy blooms bright, come what may.

Beneath the Heavens' Canopy

Underneath the leaves so vast,
A raccoon's jam was quite the blast.
He danced and pranced, forgot the past,
While pigeons cheered and flew by fast.

The apples rolled, a clumsy crowd,
While a shy pear said, "I'm so proud!"
The sky above was singing loud,
With melodies that drew a crowd.

A frog in top hat croaked a tune,
To woo a mouse who hummed at noon.
They moonwalked under the big balloon,
Creating smiles, morning till soon.

Grapes made jokes about the wine,
And mangoes danced, felt so divine.
In this wacky, sunny design,
Every critter laughs, how fine!

Serenade of the Gilded Grove

In the grove of shades so bright,
An owl hoots, "What a fright!"
While a squirrel sings with all his might,
And all the acorns join the fight.

The trees sway in a funky beat,
While ants parade on tiny feet.
A bear once tripped, oh what a feat!
And laughed so hard, he lost his seat.

Bananas wear cool shades by day,
While berries whisper, "Let's just play!"
A raccoon says, "I'll lead the way,
To mischief where we do okay!"

In a nest, the tweeters squawk,
As critters gather, share a talk.
They craft sweet jokes 'round the clock,
In this silly, playful rock!

The Language of Leaves

The leaves chatter in soft tones,
About the squirrels' acorn loans.
A caterpillar holds the phones,
While crickets laugh in silly moans.

A dandelion took a prank,
Spilling seeds near the river bank.
But then a breeze hit, feelings sank,
As flowers giggled, "You're quite blank!"

The sunflowers play peek-a-boo,
With the bees who think they're cool.
While butterflies, they make a coup,
And flutter like a wild crew.

In this place where green is grand,
The plants unite, a witty band.
With every leaf, they share their brand,
Of fun and joy across the land!

A Tapestry of Green

In the realm of leaves and vines,
A squirrel stole my sandwich, oh what a crime!
The apples giggle high above,
While I chase shadows, seeking some sun's shine.

A bee buzzed past with a dance so odd,
I waved back, but tripped on my own shoelace,
The flowers chuckled, pollen in their pods,
As I sprawled in the grass, lost in this place.

The lemons looked ripe, but were truly sour,
I bit one just to test, but spat in a rush,
The tree bark grinned, growing stronger by the hour,
As I wiped my face, feeling the blush.

With laughter all around, oh what a scene,
Nature's pranks make my day so bright,
I leave the greens, with pockets of beans,
And wander home, chuckling with delight.

Echoes of Laughter

Underneath the bright blue dome,
A rabbit stole my hat, thinking it was home.
The sunbeams danced on grass so green,
While I chased my thoughts, quiet as a poem.

A robin sang tunes that made me trip,
On roots that whispered secrets from the earth,
The flowers blinked, as if in a quip,
Turning my fumble into a moment of mirth.

The wind played tricks, tickling my side,
With a gust that made my hair fly free,
I spun around in glee, no need to hide,
The trees just chuckled, sharing their spree.

As shadows grew long, I laughed with the grass,
The crickets joined in, playing the tune,
And even the clouds seemed to softly amass,
To witness the joy of my whimsical afternoon.

Nature's Gentle Hug

In the green expanse where daisies play,
A snail decided to race me today.
With humor so slow, we both shared a laugh,
I cheered it on, for it was the best way.

Butterflies fluttered in curious loops,
As I tried to dance among all the poops,
The frogs critiqued my high-kick with glee,
And joined in a concert with croaky whoops!

Fields of clovers joined in the fun,
I searched for a four-leaf but found only two.
A mischievous breeze sent me on the run,
For it blew my cap away like it knew!

But under the sun, where silliness thrived,
I rolled in the grass, embracing the day,
With laughter's sweet song, I felt so alive,
Nature's hugs are the best, come what may!

Petals in the Breeze

Petals twirled like confetti in flight,
As I dodged a bee that came by for a bite.
I tripped on a root, the ground said, 'Well played!'
Floral laughter echoed, what a silly sight!

In the shade of the trees, I found a fine seat,
To ponder my snacks and the day's silly beat.
But oh, what a surprise, a squirrel up and grinned,
And snatched my sandwich with unfiltered deceit!

The petals giggled, dancing on air,
As I chased the thief with my wild, frantic flair.
The fruits on the branches, oh, they rolled their eyes,
Joining the prank in this comedy fair.

But soon I just sat, with a laugh in my chest,
Feeding the creatures, oh, what a jest.
Under the blooms, I surrendered my woes,
With petals and giggles, this day was the best!

Beneath the Autumn Canopy

Crimson leaves dance like crazed chips,
Squirrels wear hats as they do their flips.
Branches hang low with a fruity surprise,
While apples giggle beneath sunny skies.

Beneath this show of laughter and cheer,
The breeze tells jokes that only we hear.
Pumpkins roll by, wearing silly grins,
While lemon trees plot their next playful sins.

The sun winks down on this merry scene,
Nature's antics are quite the routine.
In this playful patch, all worries dissolve,
With laughter and fruits, we joyfully resolve.

So grab a seat 'neath this vibrant display,
Join in the fun of a fluttery day.
With each silly bloom and chuckle on breeze,
Life's a grand joke amid colorful trees.

Sighs Between the Seasons

Spring whispers softly, then yawns with delight,
While winter still snores, tucked in cozy night.
Summer frolics with its bold, sunny charms,
And autumn just giggles, holding back its arms.

The trees tell tales in the faint evening light,
Of squirrels and birds having friendly fights.
Between the seasons, laughter takes flight,
With every soft sigh, a new joke takes height.

A pumpkin once claimed it was handsome and round,
Till a cheeky zucchini rolled into town.
They laughed at their shapes, oh what a sight!
In the game of the veggies, who's wrong, who's right?

As seasons keep changing, there's no cause for sorrow,
Each giggle can carry us bright into tomorrow.
So let's toast to the moments, each one a balloon,
In this wacky world spinning 'round the same moon.

Fables of the Fruit Trees

There once was a pear with an oversized hat,
It thought it was fancy, imagine that!
A peach rolled by, laughing without restraint,
Saying, "Oh dear friend, you look like a saint!"

An apple chimed in with a grin so wide,
"You look like you're ready for a fancy ride!"
Bananas just snickered, hanging in a bunch,
As grapes giggled softly, blending in their hunch.

Together they spun funny tales of the past,
Each fruit with a punchline, none meant to last.
"I swear I saw cherries stroll into a bar,
Where laughs were so loud, you could hear them from far!"

In the canopy high, each fruit has a dream,
Where giggles and fables dance hand in hand with cream.
So join in their laughter, a fruity brigade,
In the land of the trees, where jokes are well-played.

Lullabies of the Land

Under the soft glow of the moon's gentle beam,
The crickets are singing a whimsical theme.
Stars twinkle above, with a wink and a sigh,
While the carrots groove, waving green arms high.

A nightingale whispers secrets so sweet,
As tomatoes declare it's time to retreat.
They snicker and imitate, oh what a crew,
With laughter like ripples on ponds dressed in dew.

The corn's having dreams of a comedic show,
And radishes roll, laughing row by row.
"I'm a root with a purpose, a joke on the rise,
I'll sprout all my puns 'neath the starry skies!"

So nestle in close 'neath this blanket of jest,
The land hums a tune that's simply the best.
For in every whisper of leaves in the breeze,
Lies a lullaby wrapped in the laughter of trees.

Rustic Reverie of Harvest

In the field, we laugh and play,
Chasing bees that buzz all day.
A basket down, we take a break,
And munch on apples, for goodness' sake!

Silly hats upon our heads,
Imaginary crowns woven with threads.
As we dance 'round the old oak tree,
Who knew fruit-picking could feel so free?

Giggling at worms that wiggle and squirm,
With each bite, we create our own firm.
Sweet juices drip, and we get sticky,
The sun shines bright, making us quite tricky!

Then comes the time to load the cart,
With laughter that warms both mind and heart.
We promise next year we'll do it again,
But first, let's go snack—on berries, amen!

Nectar of Nostalgia

In the orchard, memories bloom,
Where apples dangle, dispelling gloom.
A ladder's creak, a playful shout,
Who knew the harvest could be such a route?

We swipe at branches like swinging fools,
Dropping fruit while breaking rules.
A pie awaits at the end of the day,
But first, let's roll in the hay, hooray!

Tasting cider, tangy and sweet,
As we dance on the ground, with bare, happy feet.
Laughter merges with nature's hum,
Who could imagine this fun would come?

A squirrel joins in, with acorn hats,
We invite him to teach us his acrobatic spats.
The sun sets slow, but spirits soar,
Recalling adventures and always wanting more!

Cradle of Earth's Bounty

Under the branches, we lay with glee,
Counting the clouds that drift past the tree.
An old farmer laughs, says, 'Stay out of the way!'
But we only giggle, who could obey?

Picking pears with a "plop" and a grin,
Every fruit tossed makes for cheeky win.
We race with the dog, who tries to assist,
But mostly just ends up in an apple mist!

Jars ready for jam that's far from bland,
With flavors so funky, they'll make you stand!
A dance-off breaks out among the vines,
With pumpkins judging our silly designs.

Even the sun starts to fade and yawn,
As we promise to return with laughter at dawn.
A harvest so wild, it's hard to believe,
In the cradle of nature, we'll always achieve!

Symphony of Swaying Branches

In this garden, a melody plays,
As branches sway in funky ways.
We hum along, with fruit in hand,
Creating a tune that's simply grand!

Dancing with peaches, they giggle and sway,
While plums roll over, what a fun display!
Comedic slips on the orchard floor,
Fruits laughing at us as we beg for more.

"Pick me next!" cried a cheeky cherry,
But tripping through leaves, it's getting scary.
With every bite, we burst out in song,
It's the sort of place where we all belong!

With baskets filled and spirits high,
Under the sun's watchful eye.
These moments together, gold-plated magic,
Harvest days here are forever fantastic!

Nostalgia of the Seasons

Once I danced with apples bright,
Plucking fruit till late at night.
Then a squirrel took my hat,
While I pondered where it sat.

Autumn leaves began to fall,
Yelling 'catch!' I took a ball.
But a pear rolled down the lane,
I tried to catch it again!

Winter came with chilly flair,
The trees wore blankets, oh so rare.
I built a fort of branches stout,
Then lost the ball—what was that about?

In spring, the blooms all came alive,
I sneezed so hard, I fell and thrived.
The bees all giggled at my plight,
As I rolled into the wild daylight.

The Language of Trees

A cherry tree whispered 'hello',
While I tripped on roots below.
The whispers turned to giggles bright,
The branches swayed with sheer delight.

Walnuts cracked jokes up high,
As acorns danced and tried to fly.
"Hold still!" I begged, feeling absurd,
But all they did was sing like birds.

Olive branches rolled their eyes,
Said I was late for pear pies.
"Come join us, dance!" they all did cheer,
I tried a twirl, but lost a shoe here.

In the grove, friendships abound,
With nuts and fruits that joke around.
Each tree's a friend with a story spun,
Laughter echoes, and we have fun!

Twilight in the Grove

As shadows grew, I took a twist,
I planned to leave, but couldn't resist.
Fruit bats chatted in a row,
"Join our game!" Oh, where'd they go?

With twilight's glow and mischief near,
I thought I'd sneak, but stepped on a deer.
He looked quite shocked, I spilled my snack,
And grapes rolled forth, no way back.

Fireflies laughed, lighting the way,
"Come on, don't be shy, let's play!"
Sprinting after bouncing peach,
I found myself in a funny breach.

As laughter faded with the night,
The trees stood tall, a comical sight.
I waved goodbye, but heard a cheer,
"Don't forget, we'll see you next year!"

Fading Light

The sun began to skip and dance,
While I tried to catch a glance.
Fruits giggled in the fading hue,
"What's so funny?" I wondered too.

In twilight's grasp, the grass took bets,
On who would fall, the apples, or the pets?
A watermelon rolled away with glee,
Leaving me in fits—oh, can't you see?

The figs wore hats, the berries teased,
"Come on, friend! You're far too pleased!"
I stumbled on branches in good fun,
Every turn felt like a run.

As darkness wrapped the grove in peace,
Nutty laughter made my heart increase.
In fading light, we danced till late,
A fruit-filled romp without a fate.

Soft Fruit

Berries blushed with shades so bright,
Twirled around in pure delight.
A peach wobbled, lost its grip,
With every laugh, I made a trip.

Pineapples wore their crowns with pride,
Tropical gossip, they never hide.
"Join our party! We'll spin a tale!"
I grabbed a slice, it began to sail.

Ripe bananas in a conga line,
Swayed to a rhythm, oh so fine.
Each fruit a dancer, they spun around,
While I clutched my stomach, laughter bound.

As summer slipped into a quiet night,
All the fruits shared a joyful sight.
In the grove, we laughed till dawn,
Thanks to the soft fruit, we all carried on!

A Canopy of Dreams

Under trees where shadows dance,
Squirrels hold a nutty trance.
Birds debate the best sweet fruit,
While caterpillars plot to hoot.

Breezes tickle leaves so high,
While clumsy bees just buzz and fly.
Frogs join in with ribbits loud,
As laughter bounces 'neath the cloud.

Apples roll and strawberries leap,
All while the sleepy branches creep.
As if the fruits begin to tease,
In a waltz with the teasing breeze.

Oh, what joy, when sunbeams laugh,
And trees become the comic staff.
In this grove, all woes are shed,
For even grass has grins to spread.

Harvest Moon Serenade

Underneath the glowing moon,
The fruit sings an off-key tune.
Pears dance with a silly jive,
Claiming they're the stars alive.

Cider flows like jokes on tap,
As rabbits form a laughing map.
In this patch of fruity fun,
Every dusk is a pun-filled run.

Bats are giggling, playing tag,
While pumpkins wear a laughing rag.
The moon chuckles, round and bright,
As veggies join the waltzing night.

In this patch of silly mirth,
Nature spins its tunes of worth.
With every laugh, the night grows clear,
Harvest time is filled with cheer!

Beneath the Blossoms' Gaze

Blossoms wink with petals bright,
While bees wear tiny hats of white.
A fox trots by, prancing proud,
As if he's in the cheering crowd.

Fruits puff up with comic flair,
As if they're posing everywhere.
Cherries blush and giggle sweet,
Challenging the apples to compete.

Nature's putting on a show,
Where earthworms perform a hip-hop flow.
Grasshoppers play the cast of jest,
This blossom circus is the best!

With blooms above, laughter below,
In this garden, joy will grow.
The world spins round with giggles bright,
In this lovely, leafy light.

Secrets Beneath the Branches

Beneath the boughs, whispers play,
As critters scheme both night and day.
A raccoon in a cap of green,
Tries to steal the show, it seems.

A turtle joins with tales of woe,
About a slug who moves too slow.
Fruits giggle with a berry blush,
As squirrels plot in hurried hush.

The shadows spin a tangled tale,
Of nuts and jokes that never fail.
In every nook, fun's tightly wrapped,
As dreams of mischief softly zapped.

So gather round, all who seek cheer,
In this leafy nook, fun draws near.
With laughter ringing in each space,
Secrets shimmer with playful grace.

www.ingramcontent.com/pod-product-compliance
Lightning Source LLC
Chambersburg PA
CBHW062107280426
43661CB00086B/303